Hello! My Name is Public School
and I Have an Image Problem

Hello! My Name is Public School
and I Have an Image Problem

Leslie Milder
and
Jane Braddock

 iUniverse®

Hello! My Name is Public School and I Have an Image Problem

iUniverse books may be ordered through booksellers or by contacting:

iUniverse
1663 Liberty Drive
Bloomington, IN 47403
www.iuniverse.com
1-800-Authors (1-800-288-4677)

ISBN: 978-1-4759-2973-7 (sc)
ISBN: 978-1-4759-2972-0 (hc)
ISBN: 978-1-4759-2971-3 (e)

Library of Congress Control Number: 2012909684

Printed in the USA

iUniverse rev. date: 07/24/2012

Cartoon by George Abbott. Printed with permission.
Cover art design by Bill Roberson at My Comm Team

Dedicated To

Scott, without you this book wouldn't exist. Thank you for pushing me out of my comfort zone and encouraging me to find my voice and make it heard. I thank God every day that you strolled into that teachers' lounge in 1996! Mom - Thank you seems too simple. Your loving example taught me how to be a good Christian, a good teacher, and a good wife and mother. Thank you for loving me and my kids like no one else ever could. Dad - You are my hero. There was a time when I thought you wouldn't be here to walk me down the aisle or to see your awesome grandkids. I'm so glad the Lord had such an amazing plan for us. Thank you for teaching me the honor in serving the public. Aunt Jane and Aunt Judy - How blessed I am to have had you as mentors in this profession since birth! Your dedication to our great profession continues to inspire me every day. I would never have become the educator I am today without you and Mom dragging me to help in your classrooms. Thomas, Grace and Mandy, I still can't believe God has blessed me as your Mother. You inspire me daily in countless ways. Thomas, what an amazing young man of faith you are becoming. I can't wait to see the big plans the Lord has for you. You are my rock. Amazing Grace, I am so proud of the young lady you are becoming. It warms my heart to watch you "mother" all of us. You have such a beautiful heart. Mandy, what joy you have brought to our lives since the day you arrived. Your sweet spirit makes me smile every day. I love your witty ways and beautiful face. Thanks guys for your grace and patience while Mom wrote this book. I love you little, I love you big...I love you like a little pig!!!

Lord, thank you for blessing me in ways that only You could imagine.

Leslie

Also dedicated to

Andy, without your encouragement these words would not have made it to the page. I am so grateful that you have helped and supported me as I chase my dreams. I love you more today than I did 20 years ago when I first laid eyes on you — I'm thankful you picked me. I love you forever! Kaitlyn, Caroline and Kendall — I am blessed to be your Mom. You all make me want to be a better everything — wife, mom, teacher, and friend. Kaitlyn — I'm so proud of you. Remember to always let your light shine and keep reaching higher. Don't forget — La Quinta doesn't mean next to Denny's! Caroline — You are one amazing kid! Watching you grow up is one of the greatest blessings of my life. I love you for always taking such good care of us. You're quite a special young lady. Kendall — Your tender heart touches mine every day. You keep those you love close to your heart and I love that about you. See? Your name did make it into the book. To my Parents, Doug and Carol Mattix — Thank you for believing that I can do anything. There has never been a doubt in your minds that I could achieve my dreams. Who knew, right? Dad — I wish you could have read our book. It's pretty plain spoken. I wonder where that came from? I know you are watching over me and are so proud. To My Heavenly Father, the Giver of all great gifts — I am grateful for the blessings I don't deserve, but that You so freely give.

Jane

Dear friend, guard clear thinking and
common sense with your life; don't
for a moment lose sight of them.

— *Proverbs 3:21 (The Message)*

Contents

Foreword

I believe teaching to be THE most noble profession. It is a calling demonstrative of the highest level of servant leadership. A profession reserved for individuals who dedicate their professional lives to helping shape young minds, prepare the workforce of tomorrow, and create a population of positively contributing adults who will help start the cycle all over again. These are special people who pour as much love into developing challenging lesson plans as they do into preparing a home-cooked meal. Professionals who think nothing of spending their own money to outfit a classroom, clothe a needy child, or help a family down on their luck.

As a proud graduate of public schools and a mother of two still on that journey, I salute every educator who has signed on and remains committed to the mission, rising above the cacophony of negative press and misinformed critics to inspire and challenge young minds. Like virtually everyone in America, I have memories and stories of teachers who touched my life. These people inspired and challenged me. People I credit for getting me where I am today. People I will never forget, like Virginia Maddox, Jan Mayberry, Jane Rice, and Hal Barkley — public educators, all.

Through this work, Leslie and Jane are raising a megaphone to the good happening in public schools and the important role educators play in that cheer. Every educator should listen. You cannot wait, nor should you depend, on news media or advocacy organizations to tell the stories you know parents and community leaders want to hear. YOU should be proud of your work and your profession. YOU are the best person to communicate the good happening in your classroom, in your school, and in your district. YOU are the person every parent trusts with the wellbeing and education of their most precious possession.

So, put on that name tag that reads "Hello, My Name Is... And I'm a Proud Educator of Your Child," pick up the bullhorn, and tell us all about it.

Linda Rutherford
Vice President of Communications and Strategic Outreach
Southwest Airlines

Proud Public School Graduate
Founding Board Member, Friends of Texas Public Schools

Preface

We rolled into the Stone Creek Settlement Bed & Breakfast in Salado, Texas on the Friday evening of Labor Day weekend armed with two laptops, enough Coke, candy, and junk food to last a week and a suitcase of knowledge (every book on anything school related and the Bible — just in case) — thanks to Scott. We were, and Scott and Andy certainly were, determined to finish our book. This book has been written all over Texas, over about the last year, as we tried to get our thoughts on the page as they came to mind. We wrote, then traded flash drives, and edited and revised each other's work. I think we would be hard pressed to identify who wrote what at this point. However, who wrote what really doesn't matter for us because we think a lot a like — two teacher types cut from the same cloth. Our writing weekend was in an old, red schoolhouse built in 1906 in Lampasas, Texas and moved here and restored. Is there a more perfect place to write a book about our schools, students, teachers, and support staff? Thank you to our "CL" friend, Stacy, who knew this place would be the ideal spot for the two of us to collaborate on this book. This has been an interesting ride and we would like to thank our husbands, families, friends, colleagues, and of course all of the students who've crossed our paths. We are energized and inspired by the incredible success happening in our schools, which is the result of those who work in our schools – custodians, librarians, diagnosticians, counselors, aides, teachers, bus drivers, facilities and maintenance crews, assistant principals and principals, police officers, nurses, cafeteria workers, central office administrators, secretaries, speech therapists, coaches, IT pros, and school board members... for the jobs you are hired to do, and the many additional duties you take on as club sponsor, tutor, chaperone, life coach, role model, event planner, cheerleader, test coordinator, advocate, hallway monitor, safety patrol, carpool management, cafeteria monitor, wardrobe consultant (dress policy enforcer), fundraiser volunteer, ad infinitum.

Be proud of your work! Be encouraged by your incredible achievements against overwhelming circumstances. Be optimistic about the future of our profession. And most of all, make hope a habit.

> **"The key is to be hopeful on purpose.**
> ***Deliberately.* Hope is a muscle**
> **that needs regular exercise."**
> — *Price Pritchett, Author*
> *Hard Optimism*

We hope you find this book to be the valuable resource we have intended it to be and that reading it will enrich your service to this great profession.

Be blessed. Keep fighting the good fight. We have the privilege of being called to do God's work in our schools.

Jane and Leslie

Introduction

This book is inspired by the many lessons we've learned as a result of founding an organization that dared to shed light on the strengths and achievements of our public schools... to give educators a rare but well-deserved pat on the back for their hard work. So much energy is focused on what's wrong with our public schools and how to fix them that we, Americans, lose sight of the extraordinary work occurring in our schools every day, thanks to millions of caring, dedicated professional educators who will stop at nothing to ensure every student reaches their potential.

Leslie and I founded Friends of Texas Public Schools as a vehicle for reminding Texans that great things are happening in their schools. While the quest to strengthen our schools is everlasting, we must celebrate achievement along the way and demonstrate respect and admiration for those who commit their lives to public service through public education. Great things are happening in our public schools across this great country! Students and educators have never been more successful than they are today, yet we are asking more of them today than we ever have in the history of

American public schooling. Critics will disagree, but that's okay. We educators know the story. We know we educate every child who comes through our doors, from the most gifted to the most severely challenged, and that, by every measure, student performance improves with each passing year. We've allowed the critics to share their warped and misleading version of our story long enough. It's time we unite as a profession and begin sharing our story ourselves... the real story.

It's no accident that America has been and will continue to be the most productive, creative, and caring country this world has ever seen. We are indebted to our public schools for this great honor.

— Scott Milder

"Our people are our single greatest strength and most enduring long-term competitive advantage."
— *Gary Kelly, President and CEO*
Southwest Airlines

Step 1
Recognize the problem

We are blessed beyond measure to live in a land where people are innocent until proven guilty. Well, most people anyway. Seems the malcontents, conspiracy theorists, and the alarmist media have created a shortage in public confidence. With the stroke of a pen or through the lens of a television camera, public school educators are labeled incompetent, liars, cheaters, thieves, and yes, even pedophiles. (We the authors do not deny that they exist in our schools, but these types are rare and should be purged from the profession when identified.)

From school teachers and administrators to school bus drivers and coaches, educators of all walks of life are guilty of something in the eyes of the public. Even when proven innocent there is still lingering suspicion that they got away with it, whatever "it" may be.

The first step in any recovery process is to recognize that we have a problem. In fact, that's half the battle, many experts say. We cannot address a problem until we have identified that problem, and our public schools have a massive problem.

If you believe everything you hear and read about our public schools, you might be thinking they have more than just one problem. Arguments have been made by very intelligent critics, reformers, politicians, and media types that our schools are actually riddled with problems and failing our students. Hollywood is now weighing in with documentaries featuring the plight of our students. *Waiting for Superman* and *The War on Kids* are just two of them. Oprah Winfrey has even jumped on the bandwagon that proclaims our public schools as abject failures. And if Oprah says it, it must be true, right?

These self-proclaimed experts, reformers, and non-fiction storytellers are even suggesting that our schools are responsible for America's decline on the world stage.

"Public schooling is the antithesis of democracy", quotes one recent documentary. This statement must be true with well-respected American personalities such as Bill Gates, Oprah, and the architects of No Child Left Behind condemning our schools as the failures they certainly seem to be.

We have a bit of a different opinion than all of these famous, brilliant types. Do our public schools face challenges? Absolutely. Do our public schools need to improve? Always. Are our public schools the failures they are so often made out to be? Of course not!

That brings us back to Step 1 of our recovery plan. Although our public schools have many challenges, we are convinced that most of them are inspired by a single, monumental, colossal, over-arching, yet simple problem – a poor image.

You've all read the headlines and heard the rhetoric:

> - U.S. children lag behind world peers
> - Cheerleaders post inappropriate photos on web
> - Public schools falling further behind
> - Nearly 1 in 10 fails assessment exam
> - First grader suspended on weapons charge
> - Today's youth are ill-prepared
> - Cheating runs rampant in public schools
> - Schools miss dropout mark
> - Official to monitor troubled schools
> - Inappropriate relationships with students reaches epidemic proportions
> - Schools top heavy, inefficient, report says
> - School spending skyrockets, performance plummets
> - Tasmanian school children outperform U.S. peers

These statements and the mean-spirited, disrespectful debate that surrounds our public schools are all part of the greatest smear campaign in American history. We are by no means conspiracy theorists. We believe Lee Harvey Oswald acted alone. We believe most people, who we call the silent majority in America, are well-intentioned and kind-hearted. It's the vocal minority, many with their own agendas, who've hijacked the debate about public education.

Since we started Friends of Texas Public Schools in 2004 we have had quite the education on this subject. Early on we were asked by a journalist if we believed there was an organized effort to undermine public confidence in our schools, and the answer at that time was absolutely not. Critics were simply misinformed, so we thought. Our answer today, after many encounters with these critics and reformers, is absolutely "yes". Smearing our public schools undermines public confidence in our schools, which makes privatization of our public schools so much more attractive. If our public schools are failing then we should redirect our energies and resources (billions of dollars) toward private options where many in this vocal minority can get a piece of this very large money pie. Also, it's easy to lay the blame for our social problems in America at the doorsteps of our public schools. The government should be addressing many of our societal problems, not the schools. Since they haven't addressed them, they'd rather pass that blame onto our schools than take responsibility themselves. When the Russians launched Sputnik, for example, there was widespread panic that America was falling behind. The easy scapegoat for our government was our schools. We simply weren't preparing students to innovate and compete.

Hence, the birth of the education crisis when New York Times education writer Fred Hechinger first pointed it out just 10 years after Sputnik. "Almost 10 years ago, when the first Soviet Sputnik went into orbit, the schools were blamed for America's lag in space. Last week, in the Senate, the schools were blamed for the ghetto riots. In each case, the politicians' motives were suspect. Their reflex reaction, when faced with a national crisis, is to assign guilt to persons with the least power to hit back. The schools, which are nonpolitical but dependent on political purse strings, fill the bill of emergency whipping boy."[1]

Our public schools, and those who've dedicated their lives to serving in them, have an unprecedented image problem. Decades of criticism that was often unwarranted, flawed reports, and international comparisons have left Americans with the underlying belief that our public schools are not performing well. It has demoralized this profession and left educators feeling unappreciated, which we believe, ironically, has actually slowed the train of progress that our critics and reformers are so hell bent on advancing down the tracks via the laser-like focus on high-stakes testing, which, by the way, does not inspire learning.

We wonder how much faster that train would move down the tracks if those working in our schools felt respect and appreciation for their efforts? How much faster would the train be moving if it was fueled with a sense of optimism and hope rather than pessimism and defeatism? What would happen if schools were free from reform-driven testing and instead free to anticipate and adapt to every child's learning journey? Hmm...

This underlying belief of poor performance held by many Americans translates into a myth of widespread failure that has provided politicians and reformers the leverage needed to "fix" many of the manufactured problems in our public schools, which has led to a sea of policy and mandates that is drowning educators and making them appear inefficient and as though they cannot stay afloat. The truth is, by all accounts and measurements, our public schools as a whole are one of the most efficient human enterprises in human history. They achieve more with less with each passing year while politicians have the honor of claiming they have not raised taxes and are cutting wasteful spending.

As teachers attempting to stay afloat in this sea of manufactured problems, we are sick and tired of being picked on. We are fed up with baseless accusations of failure. We've had it up to our eyeballs with people believing that we are failures and that our students are not successful. Great things are happening in our schools. Our public schools have never been more successful than they are today and we resent the harsh criticism leveled mostly by those with bullhorns who have no formal connection whatsoever to the education profession. Americans have a right to know their children are in good hands, and their tax dollars are being invested efficiently. We also need to remind Americans about the significance our free public school system plays in our democracy. Are there cases of failure? Of course! But rather than condemn, let's wrap our arms around those struggling schools and lift them up rather than beat them down. Let's inject a sense of optimism back into our public schools.

Our intent with this opening chapter is to get you fired up and to motivate you to take back the conversation about our public schools. We want you to understand the severity of the situation, that you and the institution of public education are under orchestrated attack for a host of reasons, and that the only way to change the conversation and strengthen public confidence in our schools is to unite and step up as ambassadors, or champions for our profession, for our public schools, and most of all, for our students. Our kids are the brightest this world has ever known and it's about time people recognize this truth.

Homework

➢ Discuss the problem identified in this chapter with at least three of your campus or department colleagues. What top three specific negative issues do you and your colleagues believe your school community faces?

➢ Reflect on a conversation you've participated in when you could have been a better advocate or ambassador for our students and profession.

➢ Start paying closer attention to the tone of news coverage and debates about public education.

Step 2
Understand the Problem

Decades of criticism and negative news reports about the anomaly of the day, the one thing that goes wrong in our public schools each day, have created a myth of widespread failure that Americans have simply accepted as truth without question. Although our public schools are performing better today than ever before, public confidence in them has hit an all-time low.

So, the million dollar question is, how do we strengthen public confidence in our public schools with so many forces working against us? This question might be more easily answered if we ask ourselves what other industries, organizations, and companies do to build their image among their audiences. They launch branding and public relations campaigns to promote the strengths of their cause, product, or service. Do any of these ring a bell?

- ➢ Live strong
- ➢ Behold, the power of cheese
- ➢ An army of one
- ➢ Got milk?
- ➢ Just do it
- ➢ Heartbeat of America

The business community has long understood the value and importance of message. Over the last five years the public relations industry has seen double-digit growth. Kathy Cripps, president of the Council of Public Relations Firms, says, "It demonstrates that public relations as a discipline is no longer a "nice-to-have" but rather a "must-have" for clients of all kinds." The business world gets it. Isn't it about time that public schools got it, too?

We believe the time has come for public relations and communications to be a "must-have" for public schools. We have to learn how to effectively communicate what is going RIGHT in our schools and how to restore the public's confidence and hope in a public school system that is achieving great things for ALL students, for every child in America, every day. We are no longer the only game in town. The weaker our image, the more likely it becomes that those who can pull their children out of public schools will place them in a private school option because private schools are perceived to be better than public schools. Hear much in the news about a private school's performance? No!!! Nobody cares. They are not funded by taxpayers so they are not news. What we hear (and don't hear) shapes our opinions and beliefs. But we digress. The weaker our image becomes, the more charter schools and homeschoolers we'll have, which is not good for those kids. Unbeknownst to those parents, most charter schools and home schooling options provide inferior schooling to the public schools. That's why we have a professional obligation to every child to strengthen our image and be sure Americans believe in the effectiveness of our public schools so they'll choose the most effective option for their children based on reality, not myth.

You might be thinking exactly what I was thinking when my husband Scott, a public relations professional, first suggested that we should add public relations to our job description. "I am shaping tomorrow today," I believe I said at that time. "What in the world does PR have to do with teaching?" Pretty sure I said that out loud.

PR for educators... really? In all of our teacher prep coursework in college, not one of them ever mentioned the subject. In education we are taught a lot about effective communication, but only in regard to the parents of students in our classrooms.... not about communication with the broader community we serve.

Here is a little pearl I have picked up being married to a PR man... When you work in education, friends, neighbors, and mere acquaintances will come to you when they have a question or comment about something school related. It doesn't matter what job you do in education. They just know that you are connected to the schools and therefore must have more information than they have about whatever is concerning them or is in the news at the moment.

Without understanding the importance of communication we may unknowingly let golden opportunities pass us by... opportunities to correct misconceptions, rumors, or erroneous information about public schools and our colleagues. Every interaction is an opportunity to perpetuate this myth of failure, or to dispel the myth... to create a sense of optimism, or to perpetuate the standard pessimism. We need to be ambassadors for our profession, our district, our school, and ultimately ourselves! No one else will. It's the only way we'll strengthen public confidence in what we do.

"Okay, Jane and Leslie, tell us more about this ambassador theory you have," we hope you're thinking about now. Thought you'd never ask! Let's start with Webster's definition of an ambassador:

Ambassador\Am*bas"sa*dor\,Embassador \ Em*bas"sa*dor\,n.

1. A minister of the highest rank sent to a foreign court to represent their/his sovereign or country [1913 Webster]

2. An official messenger and representative.[1913 Webster]

This is how we must view ourselves — as ambassadors of our profession, our cause. We are the official messengers and representatives of our public schools. Foreign ministers do not visit other countries with the purpose of carrying a message of discontent or dissatisfaction with their country. Their job is to share the achievements and virtues of their nation and to inspire respect and admiration toward their country. As Ambassadors of public education we must do the same. We must be knowledgeable about our profession and represent it in such a way that inspires trust and confidence in our public schools.

Homework

- ➢ Think about your favorite service provider... car mechanic, doctor, babysitter, dentist, church, etc. What inspires your trust and confidence in this provider?
- ➢ Identify three other industries attempting to strengthen public confidence in their product or service. What strategies are these industries using that you could use to improve the confidence in your school/school district?
- ➢ Read on!

Step 3
Demonstrate loyalty and pride
(Especially when you don't feel like it)

"This is why, I think, so many companies fail. Not because of challenges in the marketplace, but because of challenges on the inside."
— Howard Shultz, CEO of Starbucks,
in his book, Onward (p. 41)

There are many reasons "why" public education needs good ambassadors, but as educators, for us, the most important is *pride.* We are both proud products of public schools and proud parents of three public school children each. The public schools have served us, our families, and millions upon millions of Americans very well over the last century. Changing the conversation about our public schools starts with all of us who serve in our schools. It starts with the small task of going public with the pride we take in what we do.

One of our biggest pet peeves is to hear an educator say that they have encouraged a young niece, nephew, son, or daughter NOT to become an educator. WHAT??!! If we are to restore the image and reputation that once surrounded educators we must be proud of our profession! We must stand up and tell people that we are proud to be educators and that we love what we do... and encourage others to join our profession.

Sounds simple, right? Surely we've told people how much we love being teachers. Or have we? Instead of coming home in the afternoons and telling our spouses about the many good things that happened at school that day, we typically come home and talk about the one bad thing that happened. Any of this sound familiar?

> ➤ "You wouldn't believe our crazy assistant principal."
> ➤ "I had to fill out the same form seven times today."
> ➤ "Why do I have to stop everything to take attendance a second time?"
> ➤ "They won't let us have refrigerators in our classrooms any longer!"
> ➤ "Mrs. Smith has no classroom management skills. It's out of control over there."
> ➤ "These kids are out of control. I can teach them, but I can't parent them!"

While my husband Scott knew about all the great things happening in our schools because he was the public information officer in our district, he pointed out that other spouses probably didn't know all the good things that were happening. Our spouses, friends, and families love us. If we are only sharing with them the things that go wrong in our day, they'll get angry and defensive on our behalf, leaving them with a bad impression of our public schools. Then, when they go into their private sector circles and find themselves part of a conversation about our public schools, are they going to share something positive? Probably not, because we haven't given them anything positive to share! We are their only real connection to public education and if all they hear from their own spouse or family member is negative, then that's all they'll have to pass along. Why not pass along a story about an awesome kid instead? I'm not suggesting that we stop sharing our frustrations with our families. Venting is part of human nature. But, we need to recognize the damage we are doing to ourselves and to our profession by only channeling negative energy about our work. If we take pride in our profession we should also take time to celebrate our achievements with those who are closest to us.

As proud public school parents, we want to know the person who is spending eight hours a day with our child LOVES what they do. We can't speak for you, but we didn't choose education because we thought we'd make a bunch of money. We also didn't choose to teach for the short work days and long vacations so many falsely believe are the draw. Most of us become educators because we felt *called* to it. Let's face it — we do it because we love the kids, we love teaching and watching students have those "a-ha" and "light bulb" moments. Frustrating and exhausting as it may be sometimes, we wouldn't choose anything else. Jane often tells my husband when he mentions work that she's sorry he has to get up and go in to that boring office! She'll then tell him that when she gets up and goes to work that they'll be making geometric shapes with toothpicks and gumdrops. That's what we have to do. We have to take hold of every opportunity to let everyone we come in contact with know what a cool, awesome, ROCK STAR job we have!

With all the false and misleading news stories and blogs about education, can we really afford to talk badly of our own profession? People who know us and trust us will listen to what we have to say about public schools. If we perpetuate these false or misleading news reports with our own negative stories and complaints we are not doing ourselves any favors. In fact, we are making our job much, much harder. It fuels the myth that there is a mountain of things wrong in education, and the more people perceive things to be wrong, the more leaders will choose "fixing" our schools as their agenda.

We have to promote our incredible achievements. We must beat our own drum. We need to shout from the rooftops that great things are happening in our schools because it's really the only way we can counteract all the fly-by-night, magic bullet reform solutions that pretend to fix nonexistent problems... and, frankly, that distract educators from the real progress that could be made if allowed to remain focused on the task at hand.

Everyone in our profession wants to improve, to grow, to find new and better ways to teach our kids. But, that sometimes is forgotten, or lost in the tumultuous discussion and debate on public schools. We must be the ones to remind people this job is about the kids, not rhetoric. Speaking well of our profession is a matter of pride, but also loyalty.

As a first-year teacher, I read our employee handbook cover to cover! Yes, I'm that type. It contained the following poem which has stuck with me throughout my career:

Loyalty

"If you work for a man, in Heaven's name work for him. If he pays your wages that supply your bread and butter, work for him; speak well of him; stand by him and stand by the institution he represents. If put to a pinch, an ounce of loyalty is worth a pound of cleverness. If you must vilify, condemn and eternally disparage, why, resign your position and when you are outside, damn to your heart's content. But as long as you are a part of the institution, do not condemn it. If you do you are loosening the tendrils that hold you to the institution, and the first high wind that comes along, you will be uprooted and blown away in the blizzard's track, and probably you will never know why."

— *Elbert Hubbard*

We work for the public school system. It supplies our bread and butter, puts clothes on our backs, roofs over our heads. Most importantly, the public schools provide us a stage from which we get to do what we love to do, and are called to do. Standing by that institution is a matter of loyalty, of returning the favor. Bashing, criticizing, and condemning that institution serves no purpose.

Speak well of our profession.

There is no benefit to those of us who have chosen education as our life's work, or to the children who fill our schools every day, to do otherwise. To strengthen our public schools, those of us who represent them must strengthen our bond to one another and to our profession by acting and speaking in loyalty not only to the institution of public education, but also to our school leaders. We may not always agree with every decision, but we are all on the same team. Speaking ill of public education or any of your teammates is damaging to the profession and weakens public trust.

"I'm a fireman. I have the greatest job in the world. I put out fires and save lives."

We can learn a lot from our friends at the fire station. My husband Andy is a Dallas firefighter. One night at the end of a date we stopped at the 7 Eleven. On a whim we decided to buy a lottery ticket because the lotto was a gazillion dollars. We were laughing and joking with the cashier. She said to Andy, "I bet if you win the lottery you won't go back to work on Monday." Andy looked at her, somewhat confused, and said, "Well I wouldn't quit my job if I won the lottery." Cashier looked at him, perplexed, and said, "What do you do?" Andy said, and I quote, "I'm a fireman. I have the greatest job in the world. I put out fires and save lives."

What a great testimony to his profession! We could learn a lot from this small interchange. Not only did he speak well of his profession, but he bragged on it with pride! That's how we should be speaking about our profession because you know what? We are putting out a whole lot of fires and saving a whole lot of lives ourselves!

This doesn't mean we shouldn't express ourselves when we have concerns; it just means we should be aware of how we express concerns, and where. Share your concerns and disagreements internally, not outwardly, and with respect for the other party. We said it in the previous paragraph and it bears repeating: teachers, support staff, administrators, and school board members are all on the same team! Let's lift each other up whenever possible and work together to win. Loyalty to our profession is essential if we want to recapture the respect that an educator once commanded. Like hope, loyalty also requires regular exercise, around the clock.

I am a member of the education profession 24 hours a day, seven days a week.

I can learn more about the public school where my children go on a Saturday morning at the soccer field than anywhere else. As an educator when I am in line at the bank or at church, and someone asks me about something going on at my school, I have two choices. I can perpetuate whatever misconceptions the individual may have by sharing my negative, frustrated opinion, or I can set the record straight and share something positive that I have experienced recently. Adding fuel to the fire after an incident on campus doesn't serve anyone well. The best way to alter public perception of their public schools is by altering interactions with people, one conversation at a time, from what could have been reinforcement of a negative belief to creation of a positive impression. We could certainly benefit from a sudden influx of more positive impressions about our public schools! The Beach Boys pretty much summed it up years ago...

BE TRUE TO YOUR SCHOOL!

Homework

- ➢ Tell your spouse or another family member that you love your job, then tell another person the same message each day for 30 days.
- ➢ Read on!

Step 4
Celebrate

"This is a company created by its people. It is a daily celebration here of customers. It is a daily celebration of great employees. It is a daily celebration of positive things that happen."

—Herb Kelleher, Founder of Southwest Airlines,
Author of Nuts p.190

"Whatever the reason there is just not enough celebrating going on at work — anywhere... Work is too much a part of life not to recognize moments of achievement. Grab as many as you can. Make a big deal out of them."

— Jack Welch, Former CEO of GE
Author of Winning p.78

I love the above quotes not only because I believe strongly in the truth of them, but because of who said them. Jack Welch, world renowned former CEO of GE, and Herb Kelleher, founder of Southwest Airlines, the most successful airline in the world. Seriously, two of the most iconic big business leaders in the world, and both recognize that one of the necessities of creating a successful company is celebration. Public schools succeed all the time, but we let it pass without so much as a high five. Celebrations inspire, motivate, and energize. They raise morale, boost self-confidence, remove fear, reduce stress, and help us move boldly for the future. Why in the world are we beating up our educators instead of celebrating?

If a campus celebrates the good times, then when the stormy times in education come, we have shared our successes with our families and friends so they know the storm is the anomaly and not the norm. We also feel good about our school because we have been celebrating our accomplishments.

Celebrating inspires and encourages everyone to work harder and to go the extra mile to make the difference in our schools. There are many ways a campus can celebrate successes — even small ones. Our budgets are under the microscope and we know money is tight. We have some easy, inexpensive ideas for celebrating:

> ➢ A note with an early release coupon or some Coke money goes a long way to say "you're appreciated" or "I saw what you did and I recognize your effort".
> ➢ Sonic drinks one day — really it's just the ice, cup and straw — let's be honest. You can buy two liters of drinks and get the ice from Sonic; they will often donate it to schools.
> ➢ We also have done a "Caught Ya"wreath. It's a green Christmas wreath with a bow on it. When a staff member sees someone going above and

beyond, they put the wreath on their door or workspace. Send an email to the whole staff praising your colleague for their good work. The recipient then ties something onto the wreath that represents them, then passes the wreath on — essentially paying it forward.

➤ Handwritten Notes: In this day and age of electronic communication, let us not underestimate the power of a hand-written note. Especially if it arrives in your home mailbox mixed in with all the bills and junk mail!

Don't be afraid to take a great idea for a celebration to your campus administrator. Consider asking them to create a campus morale committee. Odds are they would love to have help in finding creative, low-cost ways to help celebrate staff achievements.

There is much to celebrate!

"When people are celebrated they feel better about themselves and develop more dedication and enthusiasm toward their work."
Herb Kelleher, Author
Nuts, p. 200

Let's break out the balloons, party horns and confetti — we deserve it!

Homework

➢ Select 10 colleagues you admire and send them each a hand-written note to let them know how much you enjoy working with them. Short and sweet!

➢ Find something on your campus or in your department that is worthy of celebration, then coordinate a small celebration event for your team.

➢ Read on!

Step 5
Know your strengths

You can't celebrate what you don't know about. For us to be ambassadors of the strengths and achievements of our profession, we first have to educate ourselves about them. We need to commit a few to memory and know where to find the rest. On my campus, I knew the successes of my department backwards and forwards, but nothing about our campus as a whole or any other grade levels or departments.

Find out from campus and district leaders about their achievements. Post them in a central location on your website for all to see. Write them as simple headlines. If no one has bothered to identify what they are, then do it together!

Most of us don't get a warm and fuzzy feeling from statistics. But, it's important to have a few key points of data handy. Without the facts you are just another somebody with an opinion about public schools. It is necessary to arm ourselves with the facts, statistics, and information to set the record straight with credibility. Always have your elevator speech ready, speak clearly and knowledgably in terms that people can understand.

By the way, an elevator speech is something you would say to somebody if you had 30 seconds to brag on what you, your school, district, or universe of public education has accomplished. Here is an example:

Elevator speech

"Jones Elementary is a state-recognized campus with passing rates on the English and math exams exceeding 95 percent each year for the last three years. While we are very proud of these accomplishments, we are even prouder that every student on our campus has accepted Rachel's Challenge, which is a character education program teaching kids to put others before self."

"Reputation is what other people know about you. Honor is what you know about yourself."
— *Lois McMaster Bujold*

However, we all know that the biggest successes in our public schools are the ones that simply cannot be measured on a bubble sheet. We've all had students for whom public school is a safe place to come every day, where they do not go hungry thanks to our free & reduced lunch programs, where they are not beaten down but built up, loved, nurtured, and respected. For some children school is the only place where those things happen. I'm so tired of being compared to private schools and other nations where not every child is allowed to attend. We take EVERYONE, regardless of ethnicity, economic status, gender, or IQ. Comparing public school to institutions or nations who don't isn't comparing apples to apples. I've often said that the Emma Lazuras poem that is inscribed on the Statue of Liberty should be on the front door of every public school.

**"Give me your tired, your poor,
Your huddled masses yearning to breathe free,
The wretched refuse of your teeming shore.
Send these, the homeless, tempest-tost to me,
I lift my lamp beside the golden door!"**

A free, public education is that "golden door" to a better future for millions of American school kids.

While knowing and understanding the data and being able to explain it is important, remembering to share those successes that are not so easily measured is also vital. How many of us have heartbreaking stories about children who have passed through our classrooms? I remember the first kid I had who came from a horrible home situation. I clearly remember it hitting me that my job was to make her focus solely on U.S. Government for the 55 minutes a day I had her when she was worried about what type of verbal abuse was going to greet her when she walked through the door that afternoon, if there would be food to eat, and what was going to happen to her when Mom got out of prison. People with no formal connection to our public schools need to be reminded that these kids come from a variety of backgrounds and to judge them all equally, based on the same criteria, is simply impossible. Sharing those stories and revealing the "personal" side of what we see is crucial to opening people's eyes about the realities facing public education. My days are so unpredictable, it's not unusual for me to laugh and cry all in the same day. Kids are so funny and say the greatest, most revealing things. Tell people what a blast you have at your job! Everyone loves hearing humorous stories about kids. Art Linkletter practically made a career on funny things kids say — often you don't even have to ask — they volunteer it! Priceless! Is the task at hand easy? No way — changing someone's mind and perception is hard work. But you know what? Most days teaching is no picnic either, but who loves a challenge more that an educator?

**Our colleagues and our students
are worth the effort.**

Homework

- ➢ Draft an elevator speech about your campus or department or school district and share it with your leader.
- ➢ Engage a few of your colleagues in a scavenger hunt for your campus or department's greatest achievements, then share them in a staff meeting or via an email.
- ➢ Read on!

Step 6
Stop feeding the beast

Although there are many out there attempting to undermine public confidence in what we do, no one damages our image more effectively than we do. Yes, we just said that. We educators are our own worst enemies!

"We have met the enemy and he is us."
— Walt Kelly

Not all of us are enemies all the time, but we are all enemies on a range of "at least once in a while" to "more often than not". Fortunately, most of us in education fall in on the front end of this range when it comes to our own behaviors and conversations about our profession. But, if we are a true profession of brotherhood where we have each other's backs and the back of our profession, then our antennae must always be up and searching for the inappropriate actions and conversations of our colleagues as well. Something as seemingly harmless as a tax rate comparison chart can be damaging to our image. Although the intent of such a comparison is simply to show taxpayers that their school tax rate is lower than most of their neighbors, the unintended consequence of such a comparison is making many other districts look bad. This is what we refer to as bragging at the expense of another, and since we are all on the same team we should avoid the temptation. When identifying and sharing our strengths and achievements, let's not chunk another neighboring district under the bus to make ourselves look good. The message then conveyed almost always comes across negative, looks unprofessional, and does more harm than good.

Remember, we are all on the same team! The attack is directed at the institution of public education, not at any one school district. In fact, most people are pleased with their local schools. An annual survey of public opinion about our public schools in America conducted jointly by Phi Delta Kappa and Gallup consistently demonstrates this claim.[2] (Most recently, when respondents were asked what grade they would give the public schools, only 19 percent gave them an A or B. When asked what grade they would give the school where their oldest child currently attends, that number jumps to 79 percent. So, if that's the case, then it must be all of those other schools that are failing their students, people are led to believe.

To change the conversation about our schools we can't just worry about our own district's image because we all get lumped together. That's why our conversations need to promote the whole universe of public education.

A few extreme examples.

Exactly what do we mean by keeping an eye out for words and actions that reflect poorly on our profession? The best way to explain is through example, and there are plenty of them worth noting. How many news stories have you heard about involving **inappropriate relationships** with students? What about **inappropriate photos** on Facebook or elsewhere on the Internet? When these isolated and rare instances happen, the entire profession takes a hit, not just that one educator or school or district. If an educator in New Jersey sinks below the moral standard we all hold ourselves to, and that story makes national news, it's a dark day for educators across America. It reinforces this growing belief that immorality is pervading our nation's teaching work force. Just one incident daily by one educator out of the millions who serve our schools and communities condemns the entire institution for the day. Special thanks to our friend Mary Kay Letourneau! Her story continues to make headlines and sparked a frenzy mentality of coverage whenever an educator is accused of any misconduct with a student. The tragedy is that she likely had colleagues who were well aware of her shenanigans and they chose to turn a blind eye. That's what we mean in this chapter. If you see inappropriate conduct by a colleague, confront them and/or proceed directly to a supervisor to make them aware so they can put an end to it quietly. Holding ourselves and our colleagues to the highest moral standard is a must. We must purge our profession of anyone who engages in such behavior. Notice we say purge from the profession, not from our school or district. Please don't pass your trash on to another unsuspecting district or school!

No, purge them from the *system*. Have the courage to yank their teaching certificate and suggest they exit the profession quietly, and if they don't, then we suggest letting them know that you'll have no choice but to release the information you have on them. Having the courage to purge an immoral person from our profession means accepting the risk of lawsuit. We don't care how much they sue for because no amount is worth keeping them on your payroll.

> **"What kills the skunk is the publicity it gives itself."**
> **— Abraham Lincoln**

No mercy, folks. We must police ourselves. If we suspect that a colleague is engaged in immoral behavior with a student, we MUST say something to our campus or department administrator. Most of these episodes that make the news seem to blatantly defy common sense, but inevitably, over and over again, we have colleagues who do not hold themselves to the highest moral standard. I mean really...STOP looking at **inappropriate content** on the computer. If you can't stop then that should be a clear sign that you should resign from this profession, but if you don't have the courage to do that, then, for the love of all that's holy don't do it on your district-owned computer!!! Everything we view on our district computer is logged in somewhere in cyberspace. Even if you erase your browser history and clear your cache, it's still there. Haven't you seen those police officers carrying computers out of suspects' homes, or watched an episode or two of CSI? Nothing is ever really gone! Most districts even have certain topics/words flagged so that if they are viewed on any district machine it automatically notifies the appropriate administrators. In addition, every email you send is recorded and retrievable as well. Not only can they be retrieved, but they can also be printed and given out to any person who files an open records request, and they are admissible in a court of law. Let's put an end to news stories about educator behavior gone awry.

Be professional to be treated as one.

In addition to holding ourselves to the highest moral standard, we must also remember to conduct ourselves as professionals. We are degreed, salaried members of the most noble profession on earth. While ours does not always fit the typical mold, we must still present ourselves in a professional manner. When you are out in the community and see students, greet families and students warmly. Make sure you are still wearing your "teacher hat", and showing everyone that you love what you do and don't need several margaritas in a public place to survive the weekend. Don't get me wrong; I know teachers like to have a good time. Who doesn't? Just remember that someone is always watching, or at least someone's neighbor, sister, or friend's hairdresser and might even have a photo to share of you at your event. Consider yourself always on duty when out in public. People expect more from us than the rest, and we ought to expect the same from ourselves.

Hearing somebody say they knew a person was a teacher because she was wearing "teacher clothes" annoys me to no end. Believe me, I am the world's biggest fan of a "jeans day" and definitely think it has its place. However, we must dress appropriately, neatly, and professionally regardless of how dressy or casual our attire. How we present ourselves, and the impression it gives goes a long way in attaining the respect we receive, or don't receive, as members of the professional community.

I'm not saying that men must wear a shirt and tie, ladies can't wear sandals, that men can't have facial hair or any of that nitpicky nonsense. But, there are members of our profession who, let's face it, need a makeover! Perhaps we need a teacher version of "What Not to Wear." Let's toss out the jumpers, untucked T-shirts, wrinkled, worn out clothes that don't fit. It's high time we shed "frumpy" from the image of an educator. We can be casual, comfortable, cute and professional, but it does take some thought.

Personally, I would have loved it if the staff on our campus had standardized dress, like our students. Imagine not having to think about what to wear to work every morning. Why couldn't we have several nice, collared solid color shirts or campus shirts, and khaki or solid color pants, jeans on Friday? We would all look nice, and a visitor on campus wouldn't have to guess who's on staff because we'd stand out as the professional staff members we are. Other similar service professions have standardized dress or uniforms...nurses, firefighters.... Just a thought, but what a simple, yet major way to attack that massive chunk of damage our unprofessional dress causes our image.

"Mrs. Latham must really think we are special. She dresses up for us every day."

My Mom (Mary Latham) always dressed up for school as a teacher. She took great pride in her work and carried herself as a professional. Mom typically wore a suit, hose and heels every day to work. She taught 6th grade for 33 years. I remember once the Mother of one of her students sharing with Mom that her daughter had said, "Mrs. Latham must really think we are special. She dresses up for us every day." When you stand at the front of that room, meet with a parent, or are present at a community or school event, people notice what you wear, and how professional or unprofessional you look. Hopefully, when you do dress professionally, you aren't asked if you're going on a job interview. Dress the part daily and the respect will follow.

"You never get a second chance to make a good first impression."
— *Will Rogers*

First thing people make note of during a first impression is the way you dress.

Men please take pride in your appearance. Invest in an iron or at least put your clothes through a tumble in the dryer to get the wrinkles out. Wrinkled and worn out shirts are not appropriate for work. If you have any doubts ask a teammate. They can help you with a makeover. If you have facial hair, please keep it neat and trimmed. Your chest hair has no place in the classroom. Please button up, or trim down. Special note to our coaching friends... leave your polyester shorts and knee high socks in the field house! Dress professionally when on campus and in teacher mode.

Now ladies, this is slightly more sticky for us than it is for the men. Men, feel free to skip to the next chapter, or you can keep reading for some entertainment. Again, there are things you think are common sense, yet we have all worked with a colleague that did not get the memo about not dressing like a hootchie mama when you work with people's children. *(Chances are if you are reading this book then you did get the memo, but please be on the lookout for those who missed it.)* In fact, we have both been in the position of being asked to talk to that colleague about professional dress. This is not a conversation any of us wants to have, but for the sake of our profession and its image, we must find the courage to do so. Evidently, some moms didn't tell their daughters these things and they need to be said. So buckle up — we are going there.

Please put the girls away!

Rule #1 — Put your breasts away. Anywhere you are representing education in a professional capacity is no place to have them on display. When a parent comes to school for open house, meet the teacher, or just to have lunch with their kid, the first thing that goes through their mind should be , "Oh, how nice. There's my son's teacher." It should NOT be, "Oh... how awkward. There's my son's teacher's breasts." There is no place for cleavage in the public schools.

A great rule of thumb is when in doubt add layers; add a tank top or a cami for more coverage, which is really all we are looking for here — more coverage. Always have the Mr. Rogers sweater on the back of your chair in case of a wardrobe malfunction or just cooler-than-necessary air conditioning. You know what we mean, ladies. You men probably do as well. Please stop snickering. It's a serious matter!

What happens when I bend over in this outfit?

Rule #2 — What happens when I bend over in this outfit? There is a lot of bending over in our profession... over a desk to help a student, to retrieve things from cabinets, picking up items from the floor, getting on the floor for activities. If you are wearing a loose-fitting, low-cut or scoop-neck blouse, be aware that the teenage boy who you bend over to assist on his math assignment is going to take notice. Or, that a short skirt may show more than you bargained for if you bend over to retrieve your dry erase marker. Again, this attire has no place in public school.

Hide your undies!

Rules #3 — Undergarments are essential elements of professional dress for educators, but we shouldn't see them. No one wants to see your black bra under a white blouse or your thong peeking out of the waistband of your pants. People notice and kids definitely notice and often comment. Do you want that to be the dinner conversation that evening when a parent asks about their school day? "Hello, son. What did you learn about at school today?" Dad may ask. You don't want his answer to be anything about your support gear. You may think your science experiment was more exciting, but we assure you it was not. Keep those distractions well hidden. Need we say more?

Homework

➢ Get yourself a wardrobe accountability partner! Muster the courage to partner with a colleague to review each other's professional wardrobe.

➢ Be courageous if you encounter a colleague with a wardrobe foul. Speak up and ask them to cover up, for the sake of the children!

➢ Read on!

Step 7
Act in brotherhood, always

Police officers and firefighters get it. In many cases their lives depend on it. They are brothers in service. They've got each other's backs. Always.

> **"Sisterhood and brotherhood are conditions people have to work at. It's a serious matter. You compromise, you give, you take, you stand firm, and you are relentless."**
> — *Maya Angelou*

While we would like to say the same of educators, it does exist in pockets. We don't believe educators look at themselves and their colleagues as a brotherhood. Reality is we are a family of public servants on the same team all fighting to achieve the same thing, fighting the good fight. But the nature of our jobs is to divide and conquer, to work in silos, or classrooms and offices, which makes it a bit more difficult to live the culture of brotherhood that comes so naturally to police and fire professionals. We must work harder to achieve that brotherhood. If we are to survive as a profession, we must circle our wagons and unite as one team, or brotherhood. We have got to watch each other's backs no matter what the circumstance may be. Even if accused of wrongdoing, we rally our support behind that person until evidence and a court of law lead us to do otherwise, and "otherwise" should not be talking about the convicted person in public.

It is our responsibility to defend the reputation and honor of our colleagues, and our profession. Often that will present itself as an opportunity to say nothing at all, and suggesting the person bringing it up do the same. "Can you believe Mary did that?" we might be tempted to gossip. Your answer to that question should be, "It's really not my place to judge." It serves no productive purpose to engage in a gossip session about a colleague or incident.

Never talk trash about another educator. Ever.

Let's be ambassadors, or brothers in arms. Let's not give the enemy any more ammunition to use against us. They have plenty. Let the grapevine end with you.

> **"You can't hold a man down without staying down with him."**
> — *Booker T. Washington*

I stand beside my colleagues. If I hear a rumor or criticism about someone I work with, I will always question the perpetrator (since we are using a police analogy in this chapter) so I can learn more about the source. I will then make a point of letting that colleague know what I heard so the individual can address the issue if necessary.

The same is true if an issue comes up that's bigger than any one colleague is. Involve your chain of command if you become aware of a percolating issue or if something happens that causes you to question procedure or policy. Be careful of criticizing your school or district, especially among community members. First, give the people with the direct authority the chance to make the necessary changes.

After all, you would deserve and expect the same treatment for your classroom or department. It is also standard procedure in a brotherhood to bring solutions with criticisms.

Yes, you may create some work for yourself, but in the long run you end up winning with positive public relations for your school, building respect for yourself among your colleagues, collegiality on your campus, and ultimately our profession. Become known as a positive, driving force of optimism and brotherhood on your campus. Lead the brotherhood movement.

Lead the brotherhood movement.

We are also very careful when out in public, like at the grocery store, for example. If, like us, you live in the same community where you work, there is never an incognito moment at the grocery store or the Hobby Lobby. Dress appropriately (no foul graphic T's, for example) and slap on a happy face. And be careful what you are saying! Someone may overhear you and your spouse talking about something that frustrated you that day. Save that conversation for your living room.

On the flipside, if you are out in public and you overhear someone sharing something that is clearly not true, please step in and politely set that person straight. "I couldn't help but overhear your conversation about our school's performance rating. Since I work there I thought I might share that, shocker, the reporter got it all wrong. What really happened is..."

Always try to minimize the issue. A small incident where one kid threw a French fry at another kid and got detention could easily escalate via gossip into having been an all-out food fight where three kids were hospitalized after being hit upside the heads with Granny Smith apples. "You know I was there and it really didn't happen that way," you could say. Everyone loves a "good story" — don't let it cost your school its reputation or your colleagues theirs.

"A happy family is but an earlier heaven."
— George Bernard Shaw

A smile goes a long way! Life can be difficult; our students, families and friends will disappoint us. Be known as a positive force on your campus. A kind word with some drink money attached or a note and a piece of candy can go a long way to help someone having a rough day. Keep your eyes and your heart open to your colleagues and do what you can to lift their spirits. Another great by-product of your attention to others is you also get to celebrate with them during the good times! Earn the right to celebrate with them! Celebrating the good times builds a positive school climate — plus it's just fun.

Brothers give good counsel graciously, and receive good counsel gratefully.

At some point throughout your career you will need support, advice, good counsel, and direction. It is always good practice to have at least one colleague you are "mentoring" and one who is mentoring you. But the bottom line is, be available and open to both give help and receive it too! Common sense tells you that help and mentoring is needed at the beginning of your career; however, as we've all experienced, it doesn't hurt to have a mentor, someone who can offer you guidance throughout your career. We are never too seasoned for sage counsel! Remember, just because you reach out for help doesn't mean you're not good at your job. We would argue the opposite, in fact. It takes courage and wisdom to recognize we can't possibly have all the answers. This may be one of your greatest strengths as a member of the education profession. Asking for help is a sign of professional maturity. To admit you need help is a sign of a dedicated and honest professional. This is the personality type administrative leaders want on their teams and often serve as campus or department leaders. People naturally gravitate to others whose humility allows them to seek and to give good counsel.

> **"Part of knowing our strengths and understanding our weaknesses is making a commitment to growth. People respect a leader who doesn't have all the answers as long as they can see the leader is committed to personal growth."**
> — *Tony Dungy,*
> *The Mentor Leader page 63*

Our varied personal and professional life experiences give us different ideas and perspectives. As colleagues on a campus, we each have a license to help each other succeed. We must recognize our roles in lifting each other up to be our very best. While that often comes in the form of kudos for jobs well done, it may also arrive in the more sensitive arena of constructive feedback. These discussions are seldom the most comfortable or the easiest to have, but they are necessary in a professional environment. Those who chose to serve in public education tend to be feelers and pleasers more so than confrontational types, which make this more challenging than it may be in other private sector industries.

We're not suggesting you go and fix your colleagues. That's not your job at all. However, if you see red flags flying around a fellow educator, ask questions that will lead to discoveries that may change attitudes or behaviors for the good of your school and your fellow colleague. If that subtle approach doesn't work, you may need to be more direct, or involve your leader. Often being the bad guy for the good of your school is a role you have to be willing to step up and take. A bad decision by a colleague at your school affects you too! Evading the issue enables a colleague to continue actions that are detrimental to the individual's success and well-being. Of course, the truth should be spoken in love. As colleagues, we must own our mistakes, share our mistakes, learn from our mistakes, and move on. Grace is an act of will extended unconditionally and without limits. As teammates, giving grace, accepting each other as we are, and forgiving each other for wrongdoing creates a culture of acceptance in our profession and the ability to grow as professionals.

Like parenting, it is important to show a united front. It takes an entire staff to unite for the success of your school and care for your profession's reputation.

Lift the spirits of your colleagues.

Homework

- ➢ Be alert for brotherhood code violations.
- ➢ Practice speaking well of your colleagues with others. Compliment a colleague at least once daily for 30 days.
- ➢ Invite a respected colleague to be your mentor.
- ➢ Read on!

Step 8
Be knowledgeable about the profession

We are thoroughly schooled and prepared on the "how" of being an educator in our teacher preparation program in college, but not at all about the operational side of our profession. How much do you know about school finance? Do you know what all of those acronyms mean, much less explain them? Where does the money come from that pays our salaries? Who pays the light bill and where do they get the money? Why do we need to pass a bond to build new schools? Why do we teach what we teach, and why is there so much testing involved?

> **Education's purpose is to replace an empty mind with an open one."**
> — *Malcolm Forbes*

All of these are questions about the profession we should be able to answer, and before we began this journey of ambassadorship, we couldn't answer any of them with confidence. We had no idea where our paychecks came from, nor did we know that it wasn't the local school board that mandated a fourth year of math and science on all of our Texas high school students. Turns out that was the state legislature! Our legislators passed that bill shortly after I deleted the legislative alert from my inbox begging me to go vote for an education friendly candidate over the incumbent. I'm getting ahead of myself. More about voting later!

I taught social studies, not math for a reason. Mom and Dad didn't pass a single math gene to me, unfortunately. My children are cursed with the same problem. No, I cannot help my fifth grader with her math homework. To me, school finance is the world's hardest math problem. But, I have a responsibility to have at least a working, basic understanding of how it works. To the question about where the money comes from to fund our paychecks you may have answered, "Tax dollars". You would be right, but tax dollars from *where*? Federal, state or local?

When a school district holds a bond election because they need to build or renovate schools, it cannot use that bond money for operational expenses like paying for rising costs in utilities or to give pay raises to staff, at least that's the law in Texas. Every state has its specific laws related to education funding.

The point is, that we need to have at least a basic knowledge of how our schools get their money because it is the world's most complex math problem. Regular citizens can't get their heads around it. When a neighbor or family member complains within ear shot that we don't spend enough money in the classroom, that we spend too much on superintendent salaries and football, that their school taxes are way too high, we need to be able to professionally set them straight. FYI, on average, in Texas only 3 cents of every education dollar is spent on central administration... and that includes the salaries and benefits of superintendents and all other administrators and support staff. Another interesting fact... we spend 63 cents of every education dollar on direct classroom instruction! *For a complete breakdown of the education dollar, where each penny is invested, please refer to Tracking the Education Dollar in the Appendix.*

Back to the point about bond elections and other district budget elections or initiatives.

If a school district is asking voters to consider a bond election, it means the system is attempting to care for its facilities and provide appropriate space for students and staff. Some district bond elections are driven by growth, some are driven by the need to modernize and repair older buildings; many are driven by a combination of these two. Unfortunately, because teachers and other district staff often times don't fully understand the complexity behind such an election, some will turn out and vote against a bond election because they are upset about not receiving a pay raise or because some program was cut from the budget. "Why should we spend millions of dollars on a new elementary school when we haven't had a pay raise?" some will question. But the fact of the matter is, if the election fails, they definitely won't be receiving a pay raise any time soon because the district will be scraping together every last penny it can find to keep its buildings operating.

"If you don't like something change it. If you can't change it, change your attitude. Don't complain."
Maya Angelou

Ambassadors show trust in their leaders even when they have been given good reason not to. Our leaders have information at hand that we do not, and if they are leading us down a certain path we must take it on faith that they have good reason. And, even when our leaders have broken our trust we must take the high road as ambassadors for this profession and remain loyal, at least publicly. Privately we can roll our eyes and wonder who put that idiot in charge, but publicly we must live the creed of brotherhood, which is having each other's backs... and that includes the backs of our leaders. In most cases our leaders are making decisions with a caring heart and with students in mind and with good intentions.

Here is a good example. Recently, due to budget cuts, one school district faced a budget shortfall of several million dollars. The superintendent and school board did not want a single employee to lose a job so they turned over every rock in search of cuts that could be made without a reduction in force. One of the district's budget cuts was a reduction of paid leave days. The district reduced the number of paid leave days for teachers from 10 days to five days.

Teachers should have been grateful for the effort, but instead they were outraged and retaliated by voting against their own, desperately needed bond election. The big losers in this case were the students in this district.

Are teachers paid well or not?

Salaries are another one of those issues that can take on a life of its own. We hear a lot about teachers being underpaid, mostly from politicians and media talking heads. Some teachers will complain about it some, but I don't hear many of my colleagues ever bring up the subject at all. Regardless, teacher salaries are a hot potato in the public debate about public education. Perhaps if we paid teachers better we'd get better teachers, right? Wrong! The best teachers are not drawn to this profession for high salaries, bonuses, or incentive pay checks. By the way, incentive pay is a corporate-driven movement in public education. Although the concept works in the private sector, we don't believe it will work effectively in public education because we are not motivated by money... and that's all we'll say about that.

Let's explore this teacher salary issue a bit further. I am in my 11th year of teaching, so my salary is calculated on 10 years of experience and I have a Master's degree. My yearly salary is $50,270 and the benefits I receive add up to roughly another $15,000. My daily rate is $339.04, and my contract is 187 days. If I were an employee in another profession, I would work 250 days — 50 weeks with 2 weeks of vacation — no thank you. If you multiply my daily rate by 250 days, I would make $84,760. Really? Who could possibly complain about that for an annual salary? That salary rivals or beats most private sector jobs. However, the bonus for me is I get to spend most of June and July and a bit of August at the pool with my kids. Talk about a job perk! Again, everything I just told you is common knowledge, just a few clicks away on a district's website, but it isn't presented that way to the public — all they ever hear is that we don't pay our teachers enough.

What's wrong with teaching to the test if the test covers everything we want our children to learn?

Another often misunderstood aspect of public education revolves around curriculum – what we teach and what students are learning in school. Many mistakenly believe we drill and kill students via testing and test prep, and while we definitely test students more than we should and rely too much on testing to assess progress and performance, we are not drilling and killing students in our classrooms! Most of the testing requirements are mandated by our state and federal governments, and most of those mandated tests emerge from "think tanks" and self-proclaimed reformers who have condemned our public schools as failures based on flawed data and politically motivated agendas. Oddly enough these reformers and think tank experts (think Bill Gates and other big business crusaders, uh, we mean leaders) have no formal connection to public education and wouldn't recognize the inside of a public school if they stumbled into one! This paragraph is quickly spiraling out of control because we are fed up with the uninformed and politically driven reform conducted in the name of leaving no child behind, but in reality are covers for an organized movement to privatize public education because there is so much money to be made. Meanwhile, our schools are quietly rising to the challenges of today's diverse student population while these critics and reformers continue to paint them as failures with a broad brush. And you know what the worst part of all is?

Many of us in the profession have begun to believe the rhetoric and bold faced lies ourselves!

Yes, we listen to the same talking heads on the news as our community members, and we read the same blogs, Twitter feeds, and newspapers. Thank God I work at my school where we are doing quite well! It must be all of those other schools across the nation that are failing.

Don't be fooled! By every measure our public schools have never been more successful than they are today. As ambassadors, we need to take every opportunity to let people know it. We need to share what's right with our schools, and there is plenty of it to share.

Okay, now back to the point about what we teach and what students are learning. The material we teach is set by the State Board of Education; each district is given some freedom to teach the curriculum in any order they would like. Some districts are more scripted with their scope and sequence than others, while some allow the teacher to create her or his own lessons; develop and present them in any way they would like. The skills set out by the State must be taught sometime in those 180 days. *Each state has its own system, but they don't vary too dramatically from one to the next.*

Educators spend their time creating engaging, thought-provoking lessons that teach students to think and develop the essential skills defined through the curriculum. An educator is not just making decisions about what to teach on her own. The outline is set by the state so students in one part of the state are learning the same content as students in other parts of the state. Then, we flesh out the lessons ourselves. The public doesn't understand this and many believe we are just teaching to the test to make ourselves look good. The fact is the tests pretty accurately reflect the curriculum standards established by the state, so if students do well on the state assessments then we have successfully prepared them according to the state's expectations.

Assessments are not fun for anyone. Teachers don't like giving assessment exams any more than students like taking them. They don't ask us which ones we would like to give; they don't even let us choose the date to give it. We just get the memo from above. Assessments are a necessary evil for the function of schools because they are really the only means to provide broad comparison data between schools, districts, and states. If used as intended they also provide those of us in the classroom with information about strengths and weaknesses of our individual students.

Unfortunately, our political leaders have elevated the status of these assessment exams well beyond their intent, and these exams now drive school performance ratings, which is why our federal, state, local, and school officials place so much emphasis on them. Assessment exams are no longer used as informative tools. They have become punitive in nature because if we don't meet a minimum level of performance on them our school is labeled a failure. No wonder so much time and energy is spent preparing for these exams! No one wants to be labeled as failures, especially teachers, who hold the futures of so many children in their hands.

Should money ever be tied to those results? I think not — of course that is my opinion, but it is my book after all. By linking money to the sometimes-unpredictable testing results of students, the government is discouraging teachers from sharing great teaching strategies and ideas that work, and might even be tempting them to cheat. All of those things are just bad for morale and have no place in a school environment. There are no winners, and certainly the students come out the losers.

For most parents state assessments are scary because they don't understand them. It's important to communicate just what is expected of our students on these exams. I know our state test is testing our students on some very complex knowledge and skills, and our students are rising to that challenge. We are asking more of our kids today than we ever have before and at a much earlier age. We need to make sure that people understand that as well. We should take every opportunity to share with people what is on a state exam.

Include a sample question from last year's state exam on your weekly newsletter/email home to parents to give them a sense of what their students are learning. Many of them won't be able to answer it, but their child can! Let's show people just how complex these exams are and then show them how well our kids are doing on them. These tests are a measure of what has been learned, not simply what skill has been checked off the list.

Another thing to consider communicating is *how* the tests are given. I've been in conversations with people who think we just roll up on test day and hand out #2 pencils and bubble sheets to the kids. Explain to people that this is serious business. Let them know that we have specific training on testing procedures before they ever let us near the exam booklets... That the only words you may speak on test day are scripted for you in the test booklet, that the tests are counted out in your presence and you have to sign away your livelihood saying that they can take your teaching credentials if you mess it up! To those of us who have been witness to the evolution of giving or facilitating these tests over the years it seems like common sense that people would know we don't just casually give these exams. As Chip and Dan Heath explain in their book "Made to Stick," we have the curse of knowledge.

> **"Once we know something, we find it hard to imagine what it was like not to know it. Our knowledge has "cursed" us. And it becomes difficult for us to share our knowledge with others because we can't readily re-create our listeners' state of mind."**
> — *Chip and Dan Heath*
> *Made to Stick, p. 20.*

This happens to us quite a bit in education, especially with acronyms. There seems to be quite an epidemic of "alphabet soup" lingo in "education speak" these days. AYP, NCLB, PBMAS, PEIMS, ARD, LEP, SST, TPRI, TEKS, TAKS, PDAS, PDD, PTA, IEP, LRE, ELL, ESL, ITBS, CoGAT, DRA, PPCD, EC, TPM .....somebody shoot me, it's all just TMI! We get so comfortable with this lingo that we often forget that others who may be listening think we are speaking some new foreign language. It's the Curse of Knowledge. These aren't acronyms to us, it's our professional vocabulary and often times we find we have used one so long it's no longer an acronym, but a noun and we can't even remember what it stands for. Have you ever had to ask your doctor to repeat some information he or she has just given you, but this time in plain English? That's how a parent can feel listening to us. Knowing what all the acronyms stand for and being able to explain them and their purpose in "plain English" to our parents is essential.

Also important is to understand the many, vastly diverse jobs in education. What would your school look like if the faithful custodian didn't show up? What if the bus driver decided today wasn't a good day for work? How about the secretary or the nurse? The list goes on and on. Not one of us in education can do our jobs without all of our teammates doing theirs. We all need each other. We are a family, a really big one, which means we must treat each other like family, even crazy cousin Eddie.

> **"A family atmosphere simply means, number one, that you're sincerely interested in everyone who's a part of your family. Number two, that you forgive some eccentricities, some departures from the norm, because they are a part of your family."**
> — *Herb Kelleher, Founder*
> *Southwest Airlines*

They deserve it! Thank those people who make your job more enjoyable and easier. Thank them for their loving care. Would you want to be the nurse on your campus? No thank you! They do what they do for the exact reason we do what we do, because we love it and feel called to serve. Everyone craves appreciation for the jobs they do so well. Do your best to acquire at least a rudimentary understanding of the jobs others perform on your team. And, be prepared to explain how their role serves the larger context of the educational experience. The public does not understand, and many critics refuse to accept, that teachers cannot be effective without the supporting cast. We have a friend who happens to be a school superintendent. He describes the relationship between teachers and other staff perfectly. There are really only two roles in education, he says. There are teachers, and there are those who support teachers, and he includes himself and his school board in the support staff category.

Teachers cannot succeed without the work of the support staff, much like a fighter pilot in the air who has 18 people on the ground making sure he or she is safe and equipped to succeed.

In education that ratio is closer to one-to-one, but you get the picture. Critics suggest we are inefficient because we have one person outside the classroom for every person inside the classroom. While they paint that as a weakness, we should be proclaiming that as a strength! "We wish we had a two-to-one support-to-teacher ratio, but we are incredibly efficient with the limited resources we have at hand." We should be framing the debate about public education in this light, rather than allowing the critics and malcontents to frame it as a weakness. It's a strength!

Homework

➢ Ask your principal how much the monthly utility bill is for your campus.

➢ Study your campus or department budget so that you can answer questions about expenditures intelligently.

➢ Call your district business office and tell them you want to understand where the money comes from to fund your paycheck.

➢ Read on!

Step 9
Strengthen your communications skills

"The single biggest problem in communication is the illusion that it has taken place."
— *George Bernard Shaw*

Communicating with parents is an area that most of us have had many lessons on in our college classes or in staff development. What we haven't been trained in is to consider all communication, internally with colleagues and externally with members of the community, in a public relations context... meetings, emails, phone calls, letters, Facebook messages, Tweets, blog posts, face-to-face meetings, random encounters, and such.

Thing is, one of the few professions that have experienced sustained growth over the long haul is public relations. We wrote about this earlier in the book but we can't emphasize it enough. Over the last five years the public relations industry has seen double-digit growth. Kathy Cripps, president of the Council of Public Relations Firms says, "It demonstrates that public relations as a discipline is no longer a "nice-to-have" but rather a "must-have" for clients of all kinds." The business world gets it. Isn't it about time that public schools got it, too?

Businesses have learned that they must communicate their story with their customers and prospects to gain competitive advantage. Customers feel an allegiance to a brand. Therefore, it is ever more critical to protect the reputation of that brand. What does this mean for public school educators? It means we must be champions for our brand, 24 hours a day and seven days a week! We must be ambassadors in everything we say and do, which means our connections with parents and other community members must be high caliber, professional grade. How is that for a segue to a brief discussion about several of the most popular methods of connecting with your parents and community?

First, establish a professional relationship with your students' parents

Although you may develop friendly relationships with parents, when a community member has a child in our class we should treat that as a professional relationship. I always refer to my parents as Mr. & Mrs. Darling, for example. I don't call them by their first name, even if they ask. They are not my friends and should not be referred to so casually. I am a professional educator. We have a professional relationship. Therefore, I expect them to call me Mrs. Braddock and I expect they should expect the same from me.

Be accessible and responsive!

I always respond to any type of message within 24 hours during the school week. On the weekends, I usually read emails Sunday evening. I also try to let my parents know about my system so there are no misunderstandings. If too much time goes by with an angry parent, that individual can begin to really stew and get angry and could potentially involve others. I am a teacher no matter where I go. Sometimes that means I have to answer an educational question at the soccer field or the grocery store. All of my willingness and accessibility benefits my school, my district, my profession and me. I recently had a discussion with my local school board member about budgets in our local grocery store. Teaching is not just a profession; it's who I am. I can't and shouldn't leave that in my classroom at the end of the school day.

The blessing and curse of email

With the advancement of email, Twitter and texting, communicating with parents has never been easier. We can send an email to our entire class of parents with the stroke of just a few keys. This ease can work with you or against you depending on how you use it. When sending a group email, for example, always send it to yourself and blind copy your parent list. One upset parent doesn't need access to your class email list. A weekly email with educational concepts for the week, homework assignments and any other notes of interest is always a good idea. You cannot count on your students to convey what is going on to their parents. Some students will, but many won't. Parents like to be informed. The more information we share with parents, the better. Knowing what is going on at school is comforting to a parent and can alleviate any fears or concerns.

Phone calls

I also try to contact my parents with a complimentary phone call whenever possible. I love calling parents to let them know what their child is doing well. Such a gesture is fairly rare in this world, and any positive reinforcement of their belief that their child is awesome goes a long, long way. I will always make these calls before dinner so they can brag on their child at the dinner table. If I need to make a call to report something negative, I make that call after dinner. I don't want to turn a positive family moment like dinner into a downer for them. In this age of technology it is easy to overlook the simple and personal act of making a phone call.

Make your messages brief and professional

I send a postcard to each student at least once during each term. You can ask your data clerk to print you labels for your students. I have had parents tell me that my postcard hung on their refrigerator all year. It really goes a long way for your positive PR, and doesn't take that much of your time.

Keep your emails and other notes home as brief as possible. The more you put in print the more you are responsible for and the more they can be misconstrued. Don't be vague, get to the point, tell them what they need to know and be done with it. Stay away from declarative words like *always and never*. It is also vital to speak professionally with parents. With the advancement and social acceptance of text messaging, I understand that it is easier and quicker to abbreviate and use acronyms but that type of communication is not appropriate for a professional relationship. If you want to be treated like a professional, you have to present yourself as one! Begin your communication with a proper greeting, get to the point, thank them for their support and help with the issue and use a proper closing. Clear, concise communication is the goal of your messages.

If you are sending an email that could be taken the wrong way and there usually is a wrong way, ask someone else to read it before clicking the send button, or don't send it and make a phone call instead. Another option is to let the email rest, send it to drafts and come back to it in an hour or so. When you get a lengthy email from a parent, don't try to respond to every issue, chose one that you think is the safest and keep your reply brief. They usually just need to vent or have someone listen, and don't expect each issue to be addressed, and likely have forgotten most of those other issues anyway. Often times the best response to an email like this is a phone call. They'll appreciate the effort and you avoid saying anything in a reply that could be taken the wrong way.

Proofread for typos and tone

Remember to run a spelling and grammar check and proofread one last time before sending anything. Don't just proofread for errors, but also for tone. Since written communication is only words, you don't have knowledge of the author's intended tone. Messages can often be misinterpreted.

Spelling and grammar are important. When you represent an institution of learning and teaching, casual mistakes in spelling, grammar and punctuation are never acceptable. We are held to a higher standard in this arena than the average Joe. *In fact, we must hold ourselves to a higher standard in every aspect of life.*

As an unfortunate New York assistant principal discovered, a parent letter written in haste, anger, and frustration made national news because it was fraught with errors. What an embarrassing and painful lesson for this administrator and for public school educators everywhere.

A good rule of thumb whenever you send a letter home, an email or leave a voicemail message is to simply give it the "national news test." Ask yourself, "If this ends up on the national evening news how am I going to look?"

What about Facebook and Twitter?

Facebook and Twitter are wonderful communication tools. Facebook lends itself to keeping tabs on other's vacations, children, and activity. However, it also lends itself to keeping tabs on YOUR vacations, children and activity. Districts everywhere are scrambling to create appropriate social media policy. Check your district's policy first. I have made it a personal "rule" not to friend a parent of a student in my grade level. However, they are still able to see your pictures and activities unless you have your privacy turned on. I'm told it's called "creeping". Try it out, pick someone you don't know and aren't friends with, but have a mutual friend, and look through their pictures. Again, one picture or negative comment can damage your professional image and the reputation of your school, your district, and your profession.

However, there is a great deal of potential for us as educators in using social media professionally. One district we work with has several grade level teams with Facebook pages. For example, the "5th grade team at Whomever T. Smith Elementary" has a page that parents can "like" that will give them frequent bits of information regarding upcoming events, assignments, celebrations, and information. It is important to note that these are closed pages, meaning they can only be seen by those the teacher invites to join the page. Facebook pages are just one more way to connect with parents and help them feel engaged in their child's education. And, it shows that we are knowledgeable and effectively using the latest technology, which lets your parents and community know we are sophisticated professionals. Facebook is also one more way for us to share all the amazing things happening in our classrooms.

Twitter is a great tool for sharing brief messages with parents. Be warned! Do not use your personal Twitter account. Create a separate, professional Twitter account and keep it that way, posting only items of professional interest. They need to know what is going on in your classroom, not what you did over the weekend. Portray yourself as the professional you want to be.

Make sure your parents know how to follow you. Not all parents will follow you on Twitter, and not all will tune in through Facebook either. The message here is to use multiple mediums (Facebook, Twitter, email, phone calls, newsletters, etc...) so that you are increasing your chances of reaching everyone. People like to receive their information differently. Some are

Facebook junkies, but some refuse to join Facebook. Some are traditional types, preferring a phone call or letter home. And some, like me, get all of their news via Twitter feed.

Parent homework carries a message!

Be careful with homework and big projects. While both are vital to a well-rounded education, nothing has the potential to send your community into a tirade about their public schools faster than a poorly designed assignment. It's not necessarily the big television news story about the crisis in education that weakens public confidence in the public schools, although that certainly contributes. It's the neighborhood chatter among parents about an unclear assignment that is so complex that no elementary school student could possibly complete alone, and thus becomes parent homework. Nothing can frustrate a parent faster than trying to help a child with homework or a project. We are not suggesting you avoid homework. But, we do want to emphasize the importance of making absolutely certain that you have clearly covered all directions and expectations necessary before you send the assignment home. Also, send home age-appropriate assignments and projects with clear, educational benefit. Once, my daughter was assigned a "math scrapbook" project that was to be done entirely at home. The directions were vague and unclear. I had trouble understanding the assignment and I am a trained, certified professional! The night before it was due I noticed that another 3rd grade mom (of twins) had posted on Facebook, "Just finished my math scrapbook x 2." I laughed at her use of "my" because we all know who does those projects, but then I happened to glance down at the comments.

Twenty-seven comments!! And the twenty-seven were not expressing their excitement over the project, or the teacher's competence. Every comment was a negative one over what one person described as a "parent project." We have to look at every assignment we send home and make certain that its educational value is worth the potential hit, a black eye to our profession's image.

"I CAN'T COME OUT. I HAVE TO HELP
MY DAD WITH MY HOMEWORK."

"I know that you believe you understand what you think I said, but I'm not sure you realize that what you heard is not what I meant."
— *Robert McCloskey*

Homework

> ➢ Create a campus, grade level, or department Facebook page for professional use only.
> ➢ Place a call to the parents of each student in your class(es) over the next 30 days and brag on their child about something they did well.
> ➢ Read on!

Step 10
Plug in to the profession's politics

"The best time to plant a tree is 20 years ago. The second best time is now."
— *Chinese Proverb*

Let us begin by saying we would NEVER tell you how to vote, or for whom. But, we must plug in to the politics of our profession! We must find a way to be part of the conversation taking place about our profession, and to take the lead in that conversation. Much of the debate about public education is being led by people who are not professional educators. Yet, these people are leading our country's efforts to reform the public school experience. Really? What do you say we have a group of astronauts reform the practice of brain surgery? Makes as much sense, right?

Whether we like it or not, politics plays an integral role in public education. We have the public's money and children, the two things closest to their hearts. If we ignore that fact, and choose to bury our heads in the sand over anything political regarding our profession, then, of course, it will be frustrating dealing with what's "been done to us" in our state legislatures. We must pay attention to what legislation is headed our way. It is a whole lot easier to express our thoughts and concerns in hopes of influencing the process before a bill gets too far than it is after it has passed. That's why being informed about the education issues facing your state lawmakers is crucial to our profession. Plug in, figure it out, and spread the word when there is important legislation on the horizon.

But wait! There's more. Perhaps even more important than plugging in when there is important legislation on the horizon is plugging in when there are no urgent matters being considered in the legislature. Politics is relationships. Relationships are built on trust. It takes time to build trust and the best time to start construction is today. It's like the old Chinese proverb that says, "The best time to plant a tree is 20 years ago. The second best time is now."

Remember to Vote!

After teaching high school government for the better part of my career, I simply don't have it in me to pass up an opportunity to remind people to VOTE!! Being a registered, informed voter makes a difference in how easy or how difficult your job in the classroom can be. Teachers have dismally low voter turnout as a profession, and therefore, we are largely irrelevant when it comes to influencing legislation. Professional associations do their best to lobby on our behalf, but we cannot put our blind faith in others and trust that they will represent our best interests. Plus, they don't carry much weight if their memberships don't show up at the polls. Re-election motivates legislators to listen. Those with the most influence are those with the highest voter turnout. We have an obligation to be engaged with those who lobby on our behalf as well as doing what we can on our own and from within our circles of influence locally.

Bottom line?

We will not be heard if we do not vote.

Now, when we do vote we need to be smart about it. If you have representation that is not representing you and your interests, who does not welcome your insights, then we need to show up at the polls and vote those people out of office. But, by the same token, if you have elected officials who are fighting the good fight for you and your community, then we have an obligation to return the favor by showing up and voting to help those people stay in office. Our responsibility as informed voters doesn't end when we get someone in office. Voting and being involved politically must be a sustained effort on our part.

Learn who your elected officials are and then communicate with them regularly, perhaps in the form of a letter from your entire campus faculty and staff. Make an effort to attend community functions where you will have the opportunity to meet those individuals who represent you. Communicating with them is essential. Having personally known many men and women who serve our state, I've learned that many of them are serving with good intent. If they vote in a way that is harmful to public education, it's most likely a result of them not understanding the implications of that piece of legislation. While we might say they should know the implications before casting their votes, we have to remember that they are considering thousands of bills in a short period of time and that it's not humanly possible to read up on every one of them. That's why they establish committees. Those who serve on the House Public Education Committee, for example, become the experts on education legislation, and many of their peers in the House follow their lead when voting on education issues. Right or wrong, that's the system. So, we must focus our efforts on those members serving on the education committee, as well as help our local legislator understand the pros and cons of voting one way or another on a particular bill so they don't simply cast their vote by party line or according to someone they look to on the education committee.

Remember, just because someone is elected to office doesn't mean they are an expert in all things, though there are those with egos large enough to believe that. Many of them are looking to the education community (that's us) to communicate openly, honestly and professionally with them in order to pass quality legislation that will improve education.

Invite your elected official to your school to talk to the students. They need to be seen by your students and colleagues as someone who works for and with them. They are not movie stars; they are real people who want to make positive changes for our state. Wow — kind of sounds like what we do! If you have a project or event going on at school that you think might interest them — invite them. I assure you, if they can come they will. A visit to a local public school in their representative district is good public relations for them and great public relations for schools! Let's get them in there to see what's really going on. If they don't know about it, if we don't reach out to them, we can't blame them for not dropping by. It's really on us to invite, inform and involve our politicians. Just like other state paid employees, our elected officials work for us.

As educators we are masters at "praise what you want to raise." Why do we not adopt that strategy with our elected officials? When they do something that helps us do our job better, or benefits our public schools, however small that may be, we need to be relentless in expressing our thanks. We don't want them to only hear from us when we have a gripe or a complaint. That's how we've earned our nickname. Yes, they have a nickname for educators. They call us WASPs. Why? Because, they believe, we are Whiny Ass School People in our approach to lobbying.

We want our elected officials to look forward to hearing from us. It would help our cause enormously if they knew, when we were calling, that they would benefit from the conversation. We don't want them to dread hearing from us, informing their staff not to put our calls through, or turning the other way when they see us coming. Taking out our frustrations on those who have been elected to represent us doesn't do our profession any good. Treating them with disrespect or anger just reinforces their impression of us as WASPs.

Take the high road even when you want to reach across the desk and strangle someone.

No one who holds an elected office is ever going to vote your way 100 percent of the time. Burning your bridge with someone because they didn't vote the way you want them to is counterproductive. Remember, we must hold ourselves to the highest moral standard. That means taking the high road even when you want to reach across a desk and strangle someone. Remain calm. Decisions regarding legislation are always complex. There are many sides and many issues to consider. Don't take it personally when they don't vote the way you wanted them to vote. Maintaining that relationship is vital and the next time they are in a position to support education, they will remember your support and the relationship you have built with them.

Homework

➢ Register to vote and remember to vote.

➢ Read the legislative action updates you receive from your district and professional associations or unions.

➢ Learn who serves as your state representative and state senator and send them each a note to thank them for their service to the state and let them know you'll be watching their voting records where education is concerned. Invite them to contact you if they have any questions about how a bill might impact your school.

➢ Read on!

Step 11
Be Outraged!

"If it bleeds it leads" is alive and well in most mainstream media outlets and among self-appointed commentators and watchdogs. Most news reporting is driven by numbers. Editors look for stories that will make good headlines. Why? To sell newspapers, to attract readers to their blogs, and to reel viewers into the newscast. News is a multi-billion dollar business. Media outlets exist to make money first and foremost. This analysis is not intended to be critical of modern media. We are simply painting a picture of today's media. Many reporters are actually do-gooders to their core, doing their best to uncover corruption and protect the public from those with power. That is one of the fundamental purposes of the "free press" granted under the first amendment of our Constitution. Unfortunately, the nature of news is negative, because readers and viewers are attracted to negative stories out of a natural, morbid curiosity.

The day's headlines are most often about something that went wrong in some segment of our society. It is the news media's responsibility to report the anomaly of the day, the one thing that stands out or doesn't fit. If a middle school receives a low performing rating from the state, the news media will single out that school rather than report on the thousands of middle schools across the state that got it right. That's how a headline like "Nearly one in 10 fail assessment exam" gets published. They could have written that to read "More than 90% pass assessment exam" but that is not cause for alarm, and therefore is not news. Good news about the strengths and achievements in our public schools is so prevalent that it is not considered news.

"Okay, Leslie and Jane, now that we know this, what do we do?" you might be asking yourself. Reporters are not looking for what went right in our schools. There is just too much to report. We need to help them by sharing great stories, heart-warming stories about students achieving despite obstacles. Keep an eye out. They are everywhere! We just need to point them out. And, though these stories are found everywhere you look in the schools and could be considered the norm, each story is unique, and therefore could be considered an anomaly if singled out.

Also, when you read an article that paints education in a negative light, say something, write a letter to the editor, call the news station, and set them straight. Conversely, when a reporter gets it right, send them a note and thank them for publishing a fair and balanced story. In today's world you can email or Facebook a reporter and let them know when they got it right or wrong. If you are contacting them about something they got wrong, be prepared to present your side clearly and concisely in layman's terms. We need to know our facts. What do all of those acronyms stand for, and what do they mean to education? I love reading in the newspaper when they publish state assessment results... who's Exemplary and who moved up or down from last year's ranking, but it is difficult for civilians, including reporters, to understand their meaning. For example, I know the difference between a subgroup's score and the overall results. It's significant. Most people don't get this difference, which is why media often times simplifies reports by publishing overall scores and averages, rather than digging too deep. We owe it to each other and our profession to be able to clearly explain the results and what they mean. There are times when it is necessary for us to respond to the media and other critics. I recently responded to the Dallas Morning News regarding an article published on the Sunday before school started that was criticizing schools for achievement gaps. We are including this response to give you an example of how to politely, but professionally challenge unfair criticism. Remember, it is not only okay to respond, but essential in today's critical environment about our profession!

Dear Editor

"This morning I dropped my baby off at her first day of kindergarten. Most people would describe their thoughts and feelings about the experience, but I want to tell you what I wasn't thinking or feeling this morning.

When I walked that sweet girl into the school, it never crossed my mind what the school's accountability rating was.

I didn't wonder what percentage of their students made commended performance.

I was never once worried about the district's dropout rate, school safety, what their economically disadvantaged sub-pop is. No, I wanted to know that someone was going to take good care of her. Teach her things she needs to know, boost her confidence and make her love learning.

She had a few tears as I left her. It was a big day after all. Before I could get to the door, there was the teacher, on her knees, arms wrapped around my child easing her fears. That is what I will remember about today. That I left my most prized possession in the care of someone who wants to be in that classroom, a dedicated, highly trained professional who has made it her life's work to make my child successful in school.

You see, I am proud to be a product of Texas Public Schools and the education I received there has served me well and I want the same for her.

I am profoundly disappointed that you would run an article that not only failed to acknowledge their achievements, but criticized them, and painted them as failures. Sending these caring people back to school with that on the front page does not inspire them or lift their spirits. It beats them up, and the children of Texas are not better off because you ran that article.

They may perhaps be worse off because you have insulted and beat up the very people who spend more waking hours with them than we do as parents.

What was blatantly obvious, that you didn't report, is the enormous success of our schools. It's ok to look for ways to improve, but first let's celebrate and acknowledge what they have accomplished. You won't find a leadership book on earth that suggests constant berating of employees motivates them to work harder, yet that is exactly what we are doing with our teachers.

No, DMN, you just looked at numbers without reading between them. And my CHILD is NOT a number.

Sincerely,
Leslie Milder

When something great is going on at your campus, call the newspaper. Send them an email with pictures attached. If we don't sing our praises, who will? Faculty and staff all over the country are doing amazing things every day in the lives of kids — tell someone. Use your campus website or wiki page to showcase special programs and activities, even those you think aren't exciting. Celebrate. Imagine being in the house with that child, when their parent opens the newspaper and sees their picture. Do you think they care that the picture is them "just" working in a workstation group or working at the computer? No, that is someone's baby. What do you think the topic of discussion around the water cooler at work the next day will be — negative or positive? Just remember, they won't know if we don't tell them. We've got to be an open book! Open the doors of your school. Invite your community to witness your work. Send them a written invitation. Let them be a part of your awesome school and what is happening there.

Homework

> ➤ Find a reason to compliment a reporter and send them a letter of appreciation for fair and professional reporting.
> ➤ Read, listen, and watch news coverage about public education. You can start an RSS feed that delivers a roundup of the day's education-related headlines.
> ➤ Invite a reporter (with your leader's approval) to spend a day on campus with you.
> ➤ Read on!

Step 12
Train your army of ambassadors

Next step is to rally your troops! Create a culture of ambassadorship in your schools. To help, we have developed an Ambassador Training Academy professional development series for all public school employees, from board members and administrators to teachers and support personnel.

The ambassador training academy is designed to change the conversation about public schools from the inside out. It addresses attitudes and mindsets, helping all members of the profession step up as ambassadors for themselves, their classrooms, campuses, district, and their profession. It is designed to unite campus and district staff around the organization's purpose and strengthen the culture of brotherhood among those who work in the schools.

The academy prepares participants to act and communicate professionally and with heart and purpose... helping them avoid common issues rooted in ineffective communication practices that inadvertently undermine parent and public confidence in their work.

Participants learn how the power of professional unity profoundly impacts the profession and why this culture of brotherhood is an essential element of any successful organization. The forces that weaken public trust and confidence in public education are discussed, as well as strategies for restoring public pride, hope, optimism, and confidence in the profession.

Why?

Optimism breeds success. It motivates, inspires, and unites. Children and teachers thrive in environments that are full of hope and encouragement. Unfortunately, there is too little optimism and too much doom and gloom, generating a perception of widespread failure, demoralizing the profession, and crippling efforts to recruit and retain quality educators.

Inspiring educators to become ambassadors will strengthen pride and public confidence in the education profession and in your schools. It will unite campus and district staff around the purpose of the organization and put distractions into proper perspective.

BONUS: A strong image of public schools promotes healthy economic development and reduces perception-based migration to private schools.

To learn more about creating a culture of ambassadorship on your campus or in your district... visit www.fotps.org, or send us an email.

Leslie Milder — lmilder@fotps.org
Jane Braddock — jbraddock@fotps.org

"I wanted to thank you for today, and for all that you are doing to help us change the culture in our District. What a major shift in thinking we're undergoing. So many huge leaps forward! I'm a big believer in the power of prayer. I don't think it's an accident that you are working with our District. I am so grateful for all that you are doing for Red Oak, and for public schools."

— *Brenda Flowers, Deputy Superintendent*
Red Oak ISD

References

➢ Hechinger, F. (1967, July 30). Schools vs. riots. The New York Times, 138. (pp. 15-16 of this book)

➢ Phi Delta Kappa/Gallup Poll. http://www. pdkintl.org/poll/docs/pdkpoll43_2011.pdf. (p. 41 of this book)

➢ Tracking the Education Dollar (February 2012), Appendix (pp. 91-94 of this book)

Authors' Appreciation

If we have learned anything while writing this book it's that writing a book is a process and there are many people involved beyond the authors. We want to express our sincerest gratitude to Steve Waddell and Mark Thomas for allowing us to develop and pilot our Ambassador Training Academy in Birdville ISD... and to Brenda Flowers, Scott Niven, and Gay Lynn Jimerson-Broom in Red Oak ISD for allowing us to evolve the program into more than we ever dreamed. This journey never would have begun without the faithful leadership of our Friends of Texas Public Schools board of directors. We are indebted to you all! Thanks also to our dear friend Linda Rutherford for being an eternal source of inspiration, and for writing our book's foreword. Special thanks to SHW Group, the founding partner and sponsor of Friends of Texas Public Schools. Their financial support, encouragement, and donation of Scott's time to get Friends started made all of this possible. Though we are told never to judge a book by its cover, we'd be proud if you did. Big thanks to Bill Roberson of My Comm Team for creating the cover image. And finally, the words on these pages are spelled and placed correctly thanks to our editor Scott Milder, and to the good work of our friends and colleagues Cindy Randle, Kandi Thomas, Erin Denny, Brad Bassett, and Shirley Neeley Richardson. So many more influenced the content in this book, but our publisher has limited this space to one page, so this is it for our shout outs. God bless!

Appendix

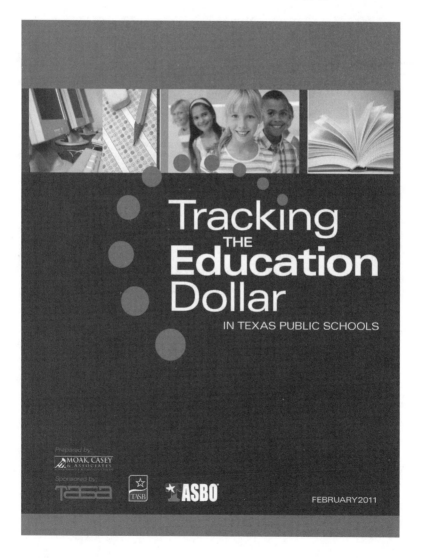

Tracking
THE
Education
Dollar

IN TEXAS PUBLIC SCHOOLS

Prepared by:
MOAK, CASEY
& ASSOCIATES

Sponsored by:
TASA
TASB
ASBO

FEBRUARY 2011

Texas Public schools spent a total of $54.4 billion in 2008–09 to educate 4.6 million students.[i] Of this total, $8.7 billion was spent on capital outlay, $4.9 billion was related to debt service, and $39.6 billion was spent on "basic educational costs."[ii] The remaining expenditures represent payments to shared service arrangements, payments into Tax Increment Financing (TIF) arrangements, and the operating costs associated with building school facilities.

Texas Public schools spent a total of $54.4 billion in 2008–09 to educate 4.6 million students.

The State of Texas collects a substantial amount of data each year regarding how school districts spend tax dollars. Each year, all school districts must account for expenditures using codes indicating the object, function, and fund for an expenditure, allowing for the analysis of what is purchased, its purpose, and the source of revenue. Detailed employment records also are provided.

The 2008–09 data indicate that public education remains a labor-intensive operation: salaries and benefits accounted for 80 percent of basic educational costs. Contracted services represented an additional 9 percent, supplies and materials were 9 percent, and other operating costs represented 2 percent.

Instruction, by function, continues to account for the largest share of educational expenditures at 61.7 percent of basic educational costs.[iii] In total, Texas employed roughly 328,000 teachers and 62,000 educational aides in 2008–09. Also included here are the salaries and benefits costs of 5,100 librarians as well as the books and other materials that can be found in Texas school libraries. The cost of instructional materials and staff development also are included in this category as instructional costs.

District operations—including facilities maintenance and operations, transportation, food service, data processing, and security—account for the next largest share at 20.8 percent.[iv] Included in this category are the salaries and benefits costs of 120,000 full-time equivalent auxiliary staff coded to operations.[v] Of these, 51,000 work maintaining Texas school buildings, 37,000 prepare and serve food for Texas schoolchildren, and 23,000 work transporting students to and from school and school-related events. Though these individuals do not work directly in Texas classrooms, they are an integral part of students' educational experience.

Instructional support accounts for the next largest share of the public education budget at 14.6 percent.[vi] Texas employed 7,400 campus principals, 9,000 assistant principals, 10,900 school counselors, and 5,700 school nurses in 2008–09.

Central administration accounts for the smallest share of all funds expended at 2.9 percent.[vii] In all, there are 12,500 full-time equivalents funded within this function. Of those, 7,700 are auxiliary staff. Superintendents, associate

2

92

superintendents, business managers, and human resource directors are all funded in this category. Also funded in this category are the cost of tax appraisal and collection, legal services, and audit and accounting services.

ELEMENTARY SCHOOL

To provide a complete picture of the inputs that compose public education in Texas, the following chart tracks the breakdown of an educational dollar from the perspective of a Texas public school student. All figures are presented in terms of pennies on the total education dollar using basic educational costs from 2008–09 PEIMS actual financial data.

Activity	Incremental Cost
The typical student begins the school day long before the first bell with a **bus ride** to school—either because she lives too far to walk or because the district has determined that unsafe conditions warrant the provision of a safe ride. She also will ride the bus home.	3¢
She arrives to find a **building that is clean and well maintained.**	9¢
The building also is **heated** in the winter and **cooled** in the summer—and the **lights** work.	3¢
Her parents know her school is made safer by district-supported **security staff**, and that if she is injured or becomes ill, she will be cared for by the **school nurse.**	2¢
She goes to class to find a **teacher** ready to begin instruction.	49¢
While in class, she has access to an **instructional aide** who supports the teacher in delivering instruction and to district-purchased **instructional supplies.**	9¢
The teacher uses a **curriculum** that is aligned with state standards and that builds on information the student learned the year before. The teacher has been **trained** regarding Texas learning standards and effective instructional practices and has access to **instructional leadership** staff who provide support.	3¢
Midway through the day, she goes to the cafeteria for **lunch.**	5¢
After lunch, she goes to the **library** to gather information for a research paper.	2¢
After school, she visits the **guidance counselor** to talk about the process of applying to and paying for college. She is given information about student loan programs, how to prepare for the SAT, and what courses she will need to take in order to be prepared for postsecondary education.	4¢
Throughout the day, she benefits from the fact that the **school is well run.** Classes begin on time, disruptions are kept to a minimum, and staff members have access to the support they need to be effective.	5¢
She also benefits from the fact that her school has access to **district-level staff** who ensure that the checks to her teachers are written on time, that all of the schools are fully staffed, and that campuses have access to the support structures they need.	3¢
At the end of the school day, she rides the bus back home—unless, of course, she stays to participate in an **extracurricular activity.**	3¢

i Charter school students and expenditures are excluded from this analysis as are recapture payments under Chapter 41 of the Texas Education Code.
ii Basic educational costs include operating expenditures (object codes 6100 through 6499) for all functions except for those within functions 71 (facilities), 81 (debt service), 61 (community services), 92 (incremental costs associated with Chapter 41), 93 (shared service arrangements), 97 (tax increment finance payments), and 99 (other). Combined, these expenditures total $1.2 billion for 2008–09.
iii Instruction includes functions 11 (instruction), 12 (instructional resources and media services), 13 (curriculum and staff development), and 95 (juvenile justice alternative education programs).
iv Operations includes functions 34 (transportation), 35 (food services), 51 (plant maintenance and operations), 52 (security and monitoring), and 53 (data processing).
v Although there were a total of 177,000 auxiliary staff employed in Texas school districts in 2008–09, 120,000 of these were employed in functions related to operations.
vi Instructional support includes functions 21 (instructional leadership), 23 (school leadership), 31 (guidance counseling and evaluation services), 32 (social work), 33 (health services), and 36 (co- and extracurricular activities).
vii Leadership includes function 41 (central administration).

3

Texas Association of
School Administrators
406 East 11th Street
Austin, Texas 78701-2617
512.477.6361 • tasanet.org

Texas Association
of School Boards
1101 Trinity Street
Austin, Texas 78767-0400
512.467.0222 • tasb.org

Texas Association of
School Business Officials
2538 South Congress Avenue
Austin, TX 78704
512.462.1711 • tasbo.org